CONTENTS

T21036

This book takes a close look at the body that breathes life into our world – the Sun. Day after day it pours heat and light on to the Earth. This makes the Earth warm and colourful, and a comfortable home for countless numbers of living things.

The Sun appears to travel around the Earth, but in fact the opposite is true. The Earth travels around the Sun. So do the other planets.

OUR SOLAR SYSTEM

SUN

Robin Kerrod

Belitha Press

First published in Great Britain in 2000 by

Belitha Press
A member of Chrysalis Books plc
64 Brewery Road, London N7 9NT

Paperback edition first published in 2003
Copyright © Belitha Press Limited 2000

Editor: Veronica Ross
Designers: Simeen Karim, Jamie Asher
Illustrator: David Atkinson
Consultant: Doug Millard
Picture researcher: Diana Morris

ISBN 1 84138 051 2 (hb)
ISBN 1 84138 756 8 (pb)

British Library Cataloguing in Publication Data for this
book is available from the British Library.

Printed in Hong Kong

10 9 8 7 6 5 4 3 2 1 (hb)
10 9 8 7 6 5 4 3 2 1 (pb)

Picture credits

Bibliothèque Nationale, Paris/Bridgeman Art Library: 15b/ET
Archive: 41l. Robert Francis/Robert Harding PL: 15t.
Arnulf Husmo/Tony Stone Images: 6-7b.
Robin Kerrod/Space Charts: front cover b, title, contents,
6tl, 7t, 9b, 10b, 11t, 12, 13t, 13c, 13b, 16t, 16br, 17, 18tl, 18cr,
21t, 21br, 22c, 23br, 25br, 27b, 28b, 29bl, 29br, 30c, 31tc,
31cr, 33r, 35bl, 35br, 36t, 37t, 39t, 40l, 42r.
The Louvre, Paris/Giraudon/Bridgeman Art Library: 14b.
Peter Menzel/SPL: 26bl.
Hank Morgan/SPL: 26br.
David Olsen/Tony Stone Images: 25t.
Powerstock/Zefa: 4-5.
Jeremy Walker/Tony Stone Images: 8b.

Some of the more unfamiliar words used in this book are
explained in the glossary on pages 46 and 47.

The Sun lies at the centre of a great collection of circling bodies that we call the Solar System. They were all born together nearly 5000 million years ago out of a vast cloud of gas and dust that once existed in our part of space.

The Sun is quite different from the other bodies in the Solar System. They are made up of rock, ice or cold gas. But the Sun is a globe of searing hot gases. If we could travel to the stars, we would find that they look like the Sun. We can think of the Sun as our daytime star.

△ Minutes before the Sun rises, it lights up the eastern sky.

Sun

Earth's orbit

Earth spins round

△ On the side of the Earth facing the Sun it is daytime. On the side facing away, it is night.

SUN TIME

The Sun provides us with a regular pattern of day and night.

Early in the morning if you look to the east, you can see the Sun rise above the horizon. By midday it reaches its highest point, and then it starts descending. In the evening the Sun sets below the western horizon.

The following morning the Sun reappears over the eastern horizon and brings daylight once more. This regular cycle of day and night gives us our basic unit of time, the day. It is properly called the solar day, or the day according to the Sun. We measure shorter periods of time by splitting the day into 24 hours, each hour into 60 minutes, and each minute into 60 seconds.

▽ In northern Norway in winter, the Sun never sets. That is why we call Norway the land of the midnight Sun.

Earth's rotation

The Sun does not really circle the Earth every day. It only appears to. The Earth rotates, or spins, in space once a day, moving towards the east. This makes the Sun appear to move towards the west.

The solar year

The Earth not only spins round in space. It also travels bodily through space in orbit around the Sun. It travels once around the Sun in 365¼ days. This period of time is called the year, or solar year. The calendar used in most countries is based on the solar year. But it is usually only 365 days long. To make up for the extra ¼ day of the solar year, an extra day is added to the calendar year every four years. This is known as a leap year, and the extra day is February 29.

Among the stars

We know that the Earth circles in space around the Sun. But from the Earth it seems that the Sun circles the Earth. The Sun appears to travel through different constellations of stars. It follows the same path each year, called the ecliptic.

THE CHANGING SEASONS

The tilt of the Earth's axis in space brings about the seasons.

The Earth spins on its axis as it circles the Sun. But the Earth's axis is not upright in relation to its orbit, it is tipped at an angle and stays pointing in the same direction in space all the time. This means that during the year the axis sometimes tips towards and sometimes away from the Sun.

The tipping axis causes a particular place on Earth to lean more towards the Sun at some times of the year than at others. The more it leans, the more heat it receives. This means that during the year the temperature at a place changes, bringing about changes in the weather, which we call the seasons.

summer Su

Following the seasons

In the tropics on either side of the Equator, there are only two seasons, a wet and a dry. But most of the world has four seasons: winter, spring, summer and autumn.

A place experiences winter when it is tilted furthest away from the Sun. In northern parts of the world, winter begins on 21 December. As the Earth moves in its orbit, its axis shifts in relation to the Sun. Northern parts of the world start to tilt more towards the Sun and warm up.

spring Su

△ **The beautiful colours of a forest in New England, USA, in the autumn.**

The Sun is highest in summer and lowest in winter.

winter Sun

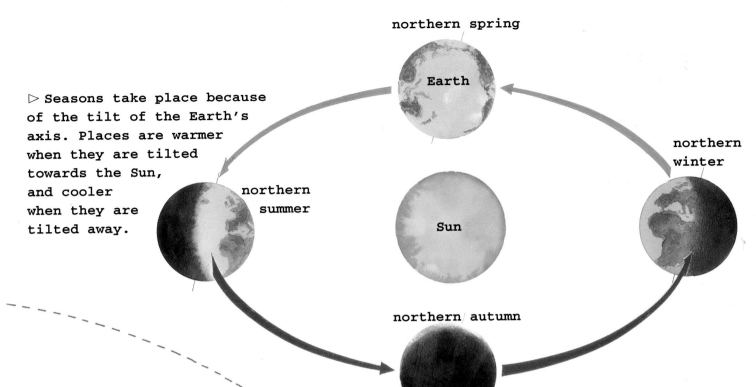

northern spring

Earth

northern winter

Sun

northern summer

▷ Seasons take place because of the tilt of the Earth's axis. Places are warmer when they are tilted towards the Sun, and cooler when they are tilted away.

northern autumn

On 21 March, spring begins. On this date the hours of daylight and darkness are the same all over the world. This is the spring, or vernal, equinox (meaning equal night).

Northern parts of the world continue heating up as they tilt more and more towards the Sun. On 21 June, they are tilted most and summer begins. Then they start tilting away from the Sun and cooling down again. On about 23 September, autumn begins. This is the date of the autumnal equinox. Northern parts continue cooling down until winter returns again.

Seasons in Australia

The dates given here are for seasons in northern parts of the world, or in the northern hemisphere. In the southern hemisphere, the seasons are reversed because southern parts of the world are always tilted in the opposite direction from northern parts.

▷ Stonehenge, near Salisbury in southern England. Ancient Britons built this monument to follow the seasons.

9

WEATHER AND CLIMATE

Energy from the Sun drives the world's weather systems.

Only a tiny fraction of the energy the Sun pours out into space – about one part in 2000 million – reaches the Earth. This energy produces the general conditions of the air around us that we call the weather. The most important feature of the weather is the temperature. This depends mainly on the amount of energy the Sun's rays provide. They heat up the Earth's surface, which in turn heats up the air above it. When the air warms, it rises. This sets up currents in the atmosphere, or winds.

beams of sunlight

Equator

△ The energy in a beam of sunlight spreads over a small area at the Equator, but over a bigger area elsewhere. This is why the Equator is warmer than elsewhere.

▽ Astronauts photographed this huge weather system above the Atlantic. It is a hurricane named Bonnie.

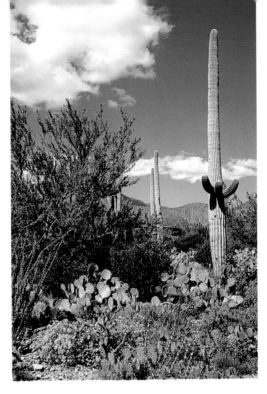

▷ Cacti growing in the Arizona Desert, USA. These plants can stand up to the hot, dry desert climate.

The water cycle

When the Sun's rays fall on seas and rivers, the water heats up and evaporates, or turns to vapour. The vapour mixes with the air and is carried away by the wind. As the air cools, the vapour turns back into drops of water, creating clouds. When the drops grow large, they fall from the clouds as rain or snow. The rain and snow find their way back into the rivers and seas, and the process starts again. This process, called the water cycle, helps determine what the weather is like.

Climate

A particular place on Earth has a similar weather pattern year after year. We call this usual weather pattern the climate. The main feature of climate is temperature. The Sun's rays do not carry the same amount of energy to every place on Earth. This is because the Earth is round and the Sun's rays fall on the surface at different angles in different places.

The nearness of the sea also affects climate. Water holds on to heat better than land, so places by the sea often have a milder climate than places inland.

Tropical rainforest
Temperate rainforest
Temperate forest
Northern forest
Scrub
Desert
Savanna
Temperate grass
Tundra
Mountains

△ Every part of the world has a different climate. Each climate suits different plants and animals.

LIFE FROM THE SUN

The Sun's heat and light make Earth a comfortable home for living things.

The Earth is unique among the planets because it teems with life. A huge variety of different kinds, or species, of plants and animals live on the land, in the oceans and in the air. They vary in size from microscopic mites to gigantic whales bigger than a house. Most forms of life on our planet need warmth, water and oxygen. They need warmth so that life-processes can take place in their bodies. They need water to carry substances around their bodies. And they must breathe the oxygen in the atmosphere to stay alive.

Just right

The Earth provides the warmth and water needed for life because it is in exactly the right position in the Solar System. If the Earth were closer to the Sun, all the water would evaporate and the temperature would be too high for living things. If the Earth were much further away from the Sun, it would be too cold for living things to thrive.

▽ **One of the Earth's tiny creatures, the 2mm long head louse. Its favourite habitat is human hair.**

Life protector
The Sun sends not only heat and light to the Earth, but also dangerous rays, such as ultraviolet (UV) rays. A layer of gas called ozone in the atmosphere blocks most UV rays, but pollution has caused the ozone layer to thin. If it thins too much, it will let through UV rays that could harm all living things.

The green leaves
of plants make food
from carbon dioxide
and water.

Sun

carbon dioxide
from air

water
from roots

◁ The Moon
has no natural
life because
it has no
air or water.

leaf gives out oxygen

Light work

Besides warmth, water and oxygen, living
things also need food. Both animals and
plants need to consume food to produce
energy. They need energy to make their
bodies work and for growth and, in the
case of animals, movement. Animals
eat plants or other animals. They
cannot make their own food.

Plants can make their own food from
carbon dioxide gas and water. They take

in carbon dioxide from the atmosphere,
and water from the ground. The two
substances combine in a chemical
reaction in the plants' leaves to
make their food, sugar. But this process
takes place only in the daytime because
it needs the energy in sunlight to make it
work. That is why it is called photosynthesis,
which means making with light.

△ The invisible
ultraviolet rays in
sunlight can burn us if
we sunbathe too long.

◁ Alligators in one
of Florida's swamps.
They raise their
body temperature by
basking in the Sun.

13

WORSHIPPING THE SUN

Ancient peoples worshipped the Sun, which kept them warm and made their crops grow.

Sun worship dates back to the earliest civilizations, which grew up in the Middle and Far East. These civilizations developed after people began to farm for food around 8000 BC. The early farming peoples worshipped the Sun because they realized how much they depended on sunshine to make their crops grow and ripen.

Sun-worship was well established in the Middle East in Babylonia and Assyria and ancient Egypt by around 3000 BC. We know this from the first written records from these civilizations. In ancient Egypt, the Sun god Ra became the most important figure.

Crossing the sky

In their mythology, the Egyptians said that Ra sailed across the sky each day carrying the Sun in a sacred boat. During the night, he sailed through the underworld, before rising into the sky again next day.

In ancient Chinese mythology, the Sun rode across the heavens in a chariot drawn by dragons. The ancient Greeks thought that their Sun god Helios drove across the sky in a horse-drawn chariot.

Later, in Ancient Greece, the god Apollo came to be recognized as a Sun god, although he was originally considered the god of light and purity.

▷ **An Egyptian woman worships the Sun god, Ra, in a painting dating from about 1000 BC. Ra is often depicted as a man with a falcon's head.**

△ **Machu Picchu, the 'lost city of the Incas' in the Andes Mountains of South America.**

Sacrifice for the Sun

Other people in the world continued to worship the Sun. Three great civilizations grew up in Central and South America that were obsessed by Sun worship. They were the Maya, the Inca and the Aztecs. They flourished until the 1500s, when they were destroyed by invading Spaniards.

The Maya, Inca and Aztecs all had powerful Sun gods, to whom they made regular sacrifices. The Aztecs carried out ceremonies to the Sun-god Huitzilopochtli. They believed that he would die and the Sun cease to shine unless he was fed each day with human blood and hearts. Sometimes thousands of people were sacrificed at the same ceremony.

Sun-day

In ancient Rome in about AD 270, the Emperor Aurelian decided that worship of the Sun would be the state religion. This continued until the Emperor Constantine adopted Christianity 50 years later. But the idea of Sun worship was not lost, for he gave the name Sunday to a weekly day of rest and prayer.

△ **Aztecs sacrificing captured prisoners at a pyramid temple. The main temple was a pyramid named Tenochtitlan. It was on the site of present-day Mexico city.**

STUDYING THE SUN

Astronomers study the Sun with special telescopes from the ground and from space.

The Sun is too bright to be looked at through an ordinary telescope. So astronomers build telescopes that project, or throw, an image of the Sun on to a screen, like a slide projector. There it can be studied and photographed. Most solar telescopes use sets of mirrors and lenses, mounted in a tall tower. A mirror on top of the tower, called a heliostat, reflects light from the Sun down a central tube. It turns during the day to follow the Sun's movement through the sky. The sunlight is brought to a focus on a table or screen in an observation room at the foot of the tower.

△ The Sun's outer atmosphere, pictured by the satellite Solar Max.

▷ The McMath solar telescope, at Kitt Peak Observatory in Arizona, is the world's biggest.

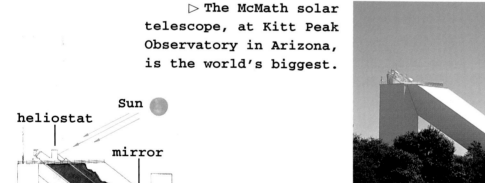

Sun

heliostat

mirror

observation room

mirror

◁ How the McMath telescope works.

▷ The spacecraft
SOHO (the Solar and
Heliographic Observatory)
studies the Sun with 12
different instruments.

Sunlight is also studied using other instruments, including a spectrograph. This produces a coloured spectrum, which shows what the Sun is made of (see page 25).

Looking at the atmosphere

Astronomers can study sunspots and other features of the Sun with solar telescopes. But they cannot study the Sun's fainter outer layers, or atmosphere. These layers become visible on Earth only during a total eclipse of the Sun, when the glaring surface is blotted out (see page 32).

But astronomers can use an instrument called a coronagraph to create an artificial eclipse. Then they can see eruptions in the Sun's atmosphere without having to wait for a real eclipse to occur.

WARNING!
Never look at the Sun with a
telescope or binoculars. It is
so bright that it will damage
your eyes and may even blind you.

Seeing the invisible

The Sun gives out many other kinds of rays besides light, such as X-rays and radio waves (see page 24). Radio waves can be studied from the ground using radio telescopes. But X-rays cannot be studied because they do not pass through the Earth's atmosphere. To study X-rays, astronomers send instruments into space on spacecraft. Space instruments can also study other radiation from the Sun that is blocked by the atmosphere, such as gamma rays and ultraviolet rays. The other great advantage of using instruments in space is that they can view the Sun more clearly and for a longer time.

DAYTIME STAR

The Sun is like the other stars we see in the night sky, but much closer to us.

▽ The Sun belongs to a galaxy (below), along with billions of other stars, like these in the constellation Cygnus (left).

If we could travel into space and look at the Sun, we would find that it looks just like a star. For that is what the Sun is, an ordinary star.

From the Earth, the Sun looks larger and brighter than the other stars only because it is much closer to us. On average, it lies about 150 million kilometres away. The next closest star, called Proxima Centauri, lies more than 40 million million kilometres away.

Enormous size

With a diameter of some 1 400 000 kilometres, the Sun is huge compared with the Earth. It could swallow more than one million bodies the size of the Earth, and it has more than 300 000 times the Earth's mass. But, compared with many stars, the Sun is tiny. Astronomers know of stars that are hundreds of times bigger.

So they call the Sun a dwarf star. In fact they call it a yellow dwarf because of the colour of the light it gives off.

The Sun is the same temperature as other yellow stars, about 5500°C. This is the temperature of the Sun's surface. It is much hotter inside (see page 20).

The Sun is really quite a small star. Stars called giants are tens of times bigger, and supergiants are tens of times bigger still.

Red dwarf

Sun

Make-up

Like all the other stars, the Sun is a ball of very hot, glowing gas. The two main gases are hydrogen and helium. These are the two lightest basic substances, or chemical elements. The Sun also contains traces of many heavier elements, including carbon, iron, silicon and magnesium. Altogether, 70 different elements have been found in the Sun.

Sun in the Universe

The Sun is one of about 100 000 million stars that form a star island, or galaxy, in space. This galaxy is one of a group, or cluster, of galaxies in our corner of space. Millions of clusters of galaxies make up the Universe.

The Sun's movement

Like the Earth, the Sun moves in two ways. It spins round on its axis and it travels bodily through space. We can see how the Sun spins by watching the dark specks called sunspots on its surface. Near the Equator, the Sun spins round once in about 25 days. Near the poles, it takes more than a month to turn round once. The Sun also travels in a long path, or orbit, around the centre of our galaxy. It takes about 225 million years to go full circle. We call this period of time a cosmic year.

White giant

Red giant

Supergiant

INSIDE THE SUN

Nuclear reactions produce the energy that keeps the Sun shining.

Years ago, people thought that the Sun was a great ball of fire. But if it was, it would burn out in only a few thousand years. Astronomers believe that the Sun has been shining for nearly 5000 million years. And they think it will carry on shining for another 5000 million years.

To find out how the Sun produces its enormous energy, we must look deep inside it, into its centre, or core. In this region, hundreds of thousands of kilometres below the surface, pressures are enormous.

▽ **Energy produced in the Sun's core travels as radiation to the convection zone. In this zone, currents of gas carry the energy to the surface, or photosphere.**

photosphere

convection zone

radiation zone

core

Sun

Temperatures in the core are also incredibly high – 15 000 000°C or more. At such temperatures, the gas hydrogen takes part in processes, or reactions, that produce enormous energy.

Nuclear reactions

On Earth, hydrogen exists as atoms, like all other chemical elements. Each atom is made up of two tiny particles. There is a proton in the centre, or nucleus, of the atom, and an electron circling around it. In the searing heat of the Sun, hydrogen does not exist as atoms. It is just a mixture

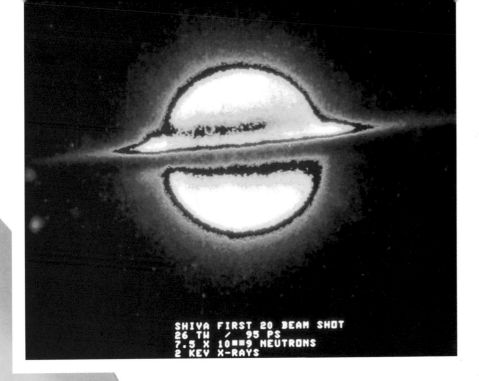

SHIVA FIRST 20 BEAM SHOT
26 TH / 95 PS
7.5 X 10■■9 NEUTRONS
2 KEV X-RAYS

△ A bright flash of energy given out in a nuclear fusion experiment carried out in a laboratory.

▽ **This stained glass window honours Albert Einstein, who devised the famous equation $E = mc^2$. It is in Grace Cathedral, San Francisco.**

of protons and electrons. Because of the heat, these particles are moving around at very high speeds. Often they collide. Sometimes protons hit one another and stick together to form larger groups of particles. These groups are the centres of another chemical element called helium. We call this sticking-together process fusion, or nuclear fusion because the protons are particles from the nuclei (centres) of hydrogen atoms.

Matter into energy

When nuclear fusion takes place, an enormous amount of energy is given out. This happens because a certain amount of matter taking part in the process is changed into energy. The scientist Albert Einstein was the first person to explain that such a change can occur. Every second in the Sun, 4 000 000 tonnes of matter are converted into energy.

$E = mc^2$

Einstein's famous equation $E = mc^2$ explains how nuclear fusion produces huge amounts of energy. E is the energy produced when mass (m) is converted into energy: c is the speed of light. Because light travels very fast, c^2 is an enormous quantity. This means that E must be enormous, too.

21

THE SUN'S FACE

Dark spots often appear on the bright, bubbling surface of the Sun.

The face of the Sun that we see is known as the photosphere, meaning light-sphere. It is the part that gives off the energy the Sun produces inside its core as heat, light and other kinds of radiation (see page 24). The temperature of the photosphere is about 5500°C.

The photosphere is a layer about 500 kilometres thick. Close-up photographs show that it is made up of boiling gases. They give the surface of the Sun a grainy appearance, which astronomers call granulation. In each granule, hot gas from below rises, gives off heat and then sinks as it cools. This process is called convection.

◁ **This false-colour photograph shows up slight differences in brightness on the Sun.**

The whole photosphere moves up and down about 25 kilometres every five minutes. Other stars vibrate in much the same way. Some change in size so much that their brightness varies noticeably. We call them variable stars.

Spots on the Sun

The photosphere is not the same all over. Particularly bright spots occur here and there. And dark blotches called sunspots appear from time to time.

The sunspot cycle

Sunspots come and go over a period of about 11 years. This is called the sunspot, or solar cycle. At the beginning of the cycle, hardly any sunspots are found. Then, year by year, sunspot numbers increase to a maximum before falling again.

Sunspots occur in regions where the Sun's magnetism is intense – thousands of times stronger than the Earth's magnetism. This magnetism triggers off all kinds of activity in the atmosphere above (see page 28).

▷ **Regions of strong magnetism are found around sunspots.**

Sunspots look like ink blots on blotting paper. They look dark because they are cooler than the surrounding surface. On average, their temperature is about 1500°C lower.

Usually, sunspots appear in groups, with two main spots. They vary widely in size. Some may measure only a few hundred kilometres across, but others may be bigger than the Earth. The large ones may remain visible for months at a time.

▽ **The butterfly diagram, a pattern that shows how the position of sunspots changes year by year (see Solar butterflies box above).**

THE SUN'S RAYS

The Sun pours out its energy as light and heat, and also as rays we cannot see or feel.

The Earth is alive because of the energy it receives from the Sun. Most of this energy comes to us in the form of light and heat. We can detect light rays with our eyes, and feel heat rays with our bodies. But the Sun also gives out energy in the form of rays, or radiation, that our bodies cannot detect. These rays include gamma rays, X-rays, ultraviolet rays and radio waves.

These rays belong to the same family of rays as light and heat rays. They are called electromagnetic waves because they are tiny electrical and magnetic disturbances. The rays are different from one another because their waves have a different length. Gamma rays have the shortest wavelengths: it would take a million million of them to measure a metre. Radio waves have the longest wavelengths: they can be up to several kilometres long. All these rays travel at the speed of light: 300 000 kilometres a second.

The Sun's dark lines
When astronomers look closely at the spectrum of sunlight, they find it is criss-crossed by hundreds of dark lines. By studying these spectral lines, they can tell what the Sun is made of. Different sets of lines are produced by the different chemical elements in the Sun.

Ultraviolet rays

Visible ligh

X-rays

Gamma rays

△ A beautiful rainbow lights up a stormy sky.

Looking at light

The light that comes from the Sun appears white, but it is not really white at all. We can see this if we pass a narrow beam of light into a wedge, or prism, of glass. The light that comes out is made up of different colours, called a spectrum. Each colour is light of a different wavelength. We often see the same colours in a rainbow. They are produced when sunlight is split into different wavelengths when it passes through raindrops. The main colours in the spectrum are violet, indigo, blue, green, yellow, orange and red.

▷ This picture of the Sun has been taken using the X-rays it gives out. The bright areas show hot regions in the Sun's atmosphere.

Infrared rays

Microwaves

Radio waves

the stormy atmosphere

THE STORMY ATMOSPHERE

Dazzling flares and fiery fountains constantly spring up in the Sun's stormy atmosphere.

Above the Sun's hot, spotty surface, or photosphere, there are layers of gases, which make up the Sun's atmosphere. There are two layers of atmosphere. The one nearest the Sun is called the chromosphere, or colour sphere, because it is pinkish in colour. The outer atmosphere is called the corona, which means crown.

◁ A tongue of fire, called a solar prominence, shoots out from the Sun. In an hour, it has travelled hundreds of thousands of kilometres into space.

Inside the atmosphere

The Sun's atmosphere is visible only during a total eclipse of the Sun, when the Moon briefly blots out the surface of the Sun.

The chromosphere is about 10 000 kilometres deep. Its lower part is cooler than the photosphere, but the temperature rises the higher up you go. The gas in the chromosphere becomes thinner higher up, too. In the corona, the atmosphere carries on thinning until it merges into empty space. But this does not happen for millions of kilometres. The corona is incredibly hot, with temperatures as high as 2 000 000°C.

The Skylab project

Studying the Sun was one of the main objects of the Skylab project in the 1970s. Astronauts aboard the US space station took more than 150 000 images using eight solar telescopes and revealed a Sun no one had ever seen before. The project had a disastrous start when the space station was damaged during its launch in 1973.

The lively chromosphere

In the chromosphere, flame-like jets of gases, called spicules, burst through from the photosphere all the time. But the action really hots up when sunspots appear in the photosphere below. The invisible lines of magnetic force found around sunspots carry gases from the chromosphere into the corona. These bursts of hot gas are called prominences. They appear as fiery fountains or great flaming arches.

Solar flare-up

The most violent activities taking place in the chromosphere are solar flares. These are explosions that take place without warning, usually around newly formed sunspots. They appear to be the sudden release of magnetic energy. When a solar flare erupts, it is the brightest feature on the Sun.

▽ **Loops of hot gas surge through the Sun's corona. This picture was taken by the coronagraph on the SOHO probe. The disc in the centre of the picture blots out the glaring face of the Sun.**

◁ **The brilliant white corona flashes into view briefly during a total eclipse of the Sun. In the corona, temperatures can rise as high as 2 000 000°C.**

THE SOLAR WIND

Streams of particles flow out from the Sun, creating a kind of solar wind.

The Sun not only gives off radiation, such as heat and light, it also gives off masses of tiny particles. They are known as charged particles because they carry tiny amounts, or charges, of electricity. The most common kinds of particles are protons and electrons. These are the particles that are found in the atoms of all substances.

The charged particles escape from the Sun, travel through its atmosphere and then flow out into space in a stream called the solar wind. The wind flows out into space in all directions, eventually reaching the outermost regions of the Solar System.

Particles in the solar wind get trapped by Earth's magnetism to form radiation belts.

Van Allen radiation belts

◁ **Solar flares like this make the solar wind blow strongly.**

Gale warnings

For much of the time, the solar wind blows gently, just like a summer breeze on Earth. It takes a week or more for the particles to reach the Earth. But the wind can be gusty, and may suddenly increase in strength to gale force, with the particles reaching the Earth in only about two days.

Wind effects

We cannot see the solar wind, but we can see the way it affects other things, such as comets. When a comet travels towards the Sun, it gives off clouds of gas and dust. The radiation given off by the Sun makes the gas particles electrically charged. When the solar wind blows, it sweeps the gas particles away from the head of the comet to form the comet's tail.

△ A brilliant display
of the aurora australis,
or Southern Lights,
seen from space.

Earth

△ The tail of the Comet
Ikeya-Seki lights up the
evening sky in 1965. It
was one of the brightest
comets of the century.

Earth's magnetic field

Coloured lights

Normally, a kind of magnetic shield protects the Earth from the wind. But if the wind blows strongly, it can make charged particles enter the Earth's atmosphere and cause magnificent displays of coloured lights, called the aurora. These displays are also known as the Northern Lights in northern parts of the world and the Southern Lights in southern parts.

Strong gusts in the solar wind can also affect the Earth's magnetism, causing what are called magnetic storms. When these storms happen, radio communications are upset, and electrical power supplies can be cut off.

THE SUN IN ECLIPSE

the sun in eclipse

Sometimes the Moon covers the Sun and plunges the Earth into darkness.

The Sun, the Earth and the Moon perform a complicated dance as they travel through space. The Moon whirls around the Earth, while the Earth whirls around the Sun. About once every 18 months or so, the Moon moves exactly into line between the Sun and the Earth and blots out the Sun's light. The Moon casts a dark shadow on the Earth and, for an instant, turns day into night. We call this a total eclipse of the Sun, or a solar eclipse.

The Moon is quite a small body, and casts quite a small shadow in space.

Its shadow only just touches the Earth during a total eclipse, and it never covers an area wider than 270 kilometres. Outside this area, people will see the Moon only partly cover the Sun. This is a partial eclipse.

Sun

During a total solar eclipse, the Moon's shadow darkens part of the Earth. The surrounding regions have only a partial eclipse and remain light.

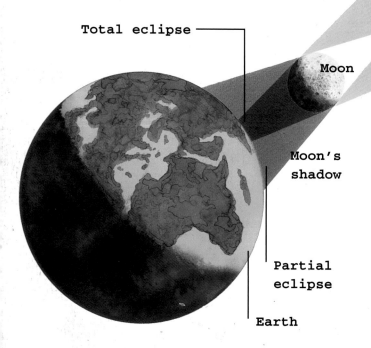

Total eclipse

Moon

Moon's shadow

Partial eclipse

Earth

Eclipse watching

A total eclipse of the Sun is a spectacular sight. It is a weird experience to find night falling in the middle of the day! Animals find it confusing too. Astronomers travel all over the world to see total eclipses for another reason. It is only during an eclipse that they can see the Sun's atmosphere. Usually, it is masked by the glaring surface of the Sun.

Four stages of a total eclipse of the Sun

An eclipse begins when the Moon first starts to move over the Sun's surface. It takes about an hour to cover it. Then darkness descends. Around the Moon, the Sun's pinkish inner atmosphere and perhaps even prominences come into view. The outer atmosphere, or corona, shows up like a milky white crown. But soon the Sun emerges from behind the Moon, and daylight returns to the Earth. An eclipse does not last long. This is because the shadow moves rapidly over the Earth as the Sun moves behind the Moon. The longest a total eclipse can last is about 7½ minutes, but most eclipses are much shorter.

1 The dark Moon slowly covers the face of the Sun.

2 Total eclipse: prominences appear around the edge of the Moon.

3 Total eclipse: the pearly white corona shows up brilliantly.

The curious coincidence

A total eclipse of the Sun can take place because of a curious coincidence. In diameter, the Sun is about 400 times bigger than the Moon. But the Moon is about 400 times closer to us than the Sun. This means that the Moon appears to be about the same size as the Sun in the sky, and can cover it up completely.

4 A 'diamond ring' appears, signalling that the total eclipse is over.

THE SOLAR SYSTEM

the solar system

The Sun travels through space with a large family.

The Earth is one of nine bodies that circle in space around the Sun. The planets form the major part of the Sun's family in space, called the Solar System.

Circling the Sun

The planets circle around the Sun at different distances, in lengthy paths, or orbits. The planet nearest the Sun is Mercury, then in order come Venus, Earth, Mars, Jupiter, Saturn, Uranus, Neptune and Pluto.

The orbits of the planets are far apart, varying from tens of millions of kilometres in the inner part of the Solar System to thousands of millions of kilometres in the outer part. The planets are held in their orbits by the gravity of the Sun. This is so powerful that it can hold on to a ball of icy rock about 2200 kilometres wide over a distance of up to 7000 million kilometres. This ball is the planet Pluto.

The planets circle around the Sun in the same direction. If you could travel to a point in space far above the Earth's North Pole and look back, you would see the planets travelling anticlockwise. Most planets travel round the Sun in orbits that are nearly circular. But Mercury and Pluto travel in orbits that are oval, or elliptical. All the planets travel around the Sun in much the same plane. This means that they and the Sun could be placed, more or less, on a flat sheet in space.

Uranus

Earth

Mercury

Saturn

Mars

Sun

Venus

Jupiter

comet

Neptune

Pluto

direction of planets

direction of planets

◁ The orbits of the planets, drawn roughly to the same scale. They occupy a region of space 15 000 million kilometres across.

▽ Some of the smaller members of the Sun's family: Halley's comet (right) and four moons of Jupiter.

Fellow travellers

Many other bodies belong to the Sun's family. Most of the planets have satellites, or moons, circling round them. Between the orbits of Mars and Jupiter there is a swarm of asteroids. They are rocky lumps, at most only a few hundred kilometres wide. Smaller still are the icy lumps we call comets.

△ One of the many huge clouds of gas and dust that exist in space. It is found in the Eagle Nebula. Stars like the Sun are born in clouds like this.

△ The Sun began to form when a cloud started to collapse under gravity. The shrinking cloud began to spin round and formed a flat disc shape.

BIRTH OF THE SOLAR SYSTEM

The Solar System was born in a vast, billowing cloud of gas and dust.

Wisps of gas and tiny specks of dust are found everywhere in the space between the stars. They form interstellar matter. In some places they gather into enormous clouds millions and millions of kilometres wide. These clouds contain many different chemical substances, but the most common substance is the gas, hydrogen.

There was once a huge cloud in space where the Solar System lies today. About 4600 million years ago, the cloud began to collapse. Astronomers think that shock waves from a nearby exploding star caused this to happen. Inside the cloud the particles of gas and dust were pulled together by gravity. At the same time the cloud began to swirl round. This continued for thousands of years, with the cloud becoming smaller and flattening out into a disc. In the centre of the disc, a ball of denser matter formed. It became very hot, and started to glow.

The infant Sun

The glowing centre of the shrinking cloud was the infant Sun. As the infant Sun continued to shrink, the temperature inside it built up until it reached more than 10 million degrees. At this temperature hydrogen atoms began to fuse (join) together to form helium atoms. Fantastic amounts of energy were released in this process, which is called nuclear fusion. For the first time, the Sun began to shine, as a new star.

◁ A planetary nebula called the Stingray.

The planets

The particles in the disc of swirling gas and dust surrounding the Sun collided and stuck together. First they formed into larger lumps that we call planetesimals. These gradually clumped together to form the planets. Many lumps were left over, and these are what we now call asteroids and comets.

▽ At the centre of the cloud, a ball of matter formed. It was the infant Sun.

Death of the Sun

In about 5000 million years, the Sun will start to die. It will expand and turn red. Then its outer layers will blow away, leaving a small, hot core. The Sun will become a white dwarf star. But in time its light will fade. The Sun will end its life as a black dwarf.

▷ The infant Sun began to shine. Matter in the surrounding disc formed huge clumps.

▷▷ In time, the clumps swept up most of the matter around them. They became the planets.

DWARFS AND GIANTS

Earth is a medium-sized planet: four planets are smaller, four are larger.

There is no such thing as a typical planet. All the planets are different from one another in appearance, in make-up, and in size. To us, the Earth seems huge. Indeed, it is bigger than its neighbours in the inner part of the Solar System, Mercury, Venus and Mars.

▽ **The nine planets, drawn to the same scale. Jupiter and Saturn are by far the biggest. The Earth is tiny in comparison.**

Jupiter

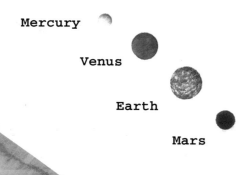

Mercury

Venus

Earth

Mars

Sun

These three planets are similar in composition to the Earth, being made up mainly of layers of rock on top of a centre, or core, of metal. This is why they are called the terrestrial, or Earth-like planets.

The giants

The Earth may be bigger than its planetary neighbours, but it is a dwarf when compared with other planets further out. The two largest ones are Jupiter and Saturn, which lie far beyond Mars. They are truly giant-sized. Jupiter's diameter is 11 times that of the Earth, and Saturn is only slightly smaller. Together, these two planets

Saturn

Uranus

Pluto

Neptune

△ Rocks litter the surface of Mars, one of the three Earth-like planets. The Pathfinder probe snapped this picture in 1997.

have more than 92 per cent of the mass of all the planets put together. Uranus and Neptune are much smaller than Jupiter and Saturn, but still dwarf the Earth.

Gas balls

The four giant planets are made up mainly of gases, particularly hydrogen and helium, and they all have a very deep and very cold gassy atmosphere. Beneath the atmosphere, there is an ocean of liquid gas. There is no solid surface at all. Beneath the ocean, the pressure is so great that the gas turns into liquid metal. Only at the very centre of the planet is there a core of rock.

But the gas giants are dwarfed by the biggest body in the Solar System – the Sun. This is also a gas ball, of course, but it is made up of gas that is searing hot.

Moons and rings

There are other major differences between the dwarf terrestrial planets and the gas giants. The four terrestrial planets have between them only three satellites, or moons. The four giant planets have between them at least 64 moons! Another feature of the giant planets is that they all have systems of rings circling round them. Saturn has the broadest rings, easily visible from Earth through telescopes. None of the terrestrial planets has rings.

PLANETS IN THE SKY

The five closest planets often shine brightly in the night.

On many evenings of the year, a very bright star appears in the western sky just as the Sun sets. But this bright object, which is called the evening star, is not a star at all. It is the planet Venus. It shines so brightly because it is the closest planet to the Earth.

Of the near planets, Mercury and Saturn are usually difficult to see. Mercury is hard to spot because it never strays very far away from the Sun in the sky. It always appears very low down on the horizon and in a light sky. Saturn can be as bright as the brightest stars, but is hard to find unless you know exactly where to look.

Mars and Jupiter are usually easy to spot. They can both become much brighter than any star and shine like beacons in the night sky. You can easily tell them apart because Jupiter is a brilliant white, while Mars has a distinct reddish glow. That is why it is called the Red Planet.

△ The zodiac constellation Gemini, the Twins. Its twin bright stars are named Castor and Pollux.

▽ The constellations of the zodiac, which astrologers call star signs. Most are named after animals.

You can see four more planets in the night sky with the naked eye – Mercury, Mars, Jupiter and Saturn. The remaining planets, Uranus, Neptune and Pluto, are too faint to be visible because they are so far away.

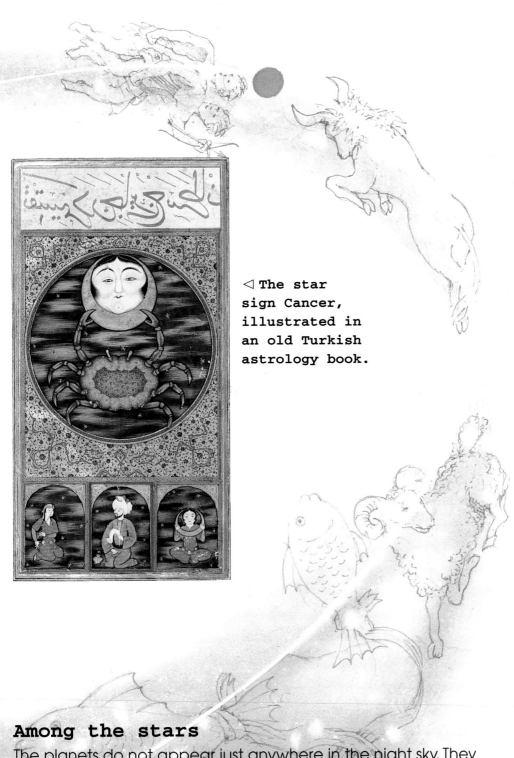

◁ **The star sign Cancer, illustrated in an old Turkish astrology book.**

Among the stars

The planets do not appear just anywhere in the night sky. They can be found only in a narrow band passing through certain constellations. This band is called the zodiac. This name means the 'circle of animals', because most of the constellations it passes through have animal names, such as Leo (Lion) and Taurus (Bull). Ancient star-gazers believed that the positions of the Sun and the planets in the zodiac affected people's characters and the lives they led. This belief was called astrology. Many people still believe in astrology, although astronomers have found no scientific evidence that there is any truth in it.

The evening star Venus appears with the crescent Moon in the western sky at sunset.

TIME LINE

2136 BC
On 22 October, Chinese astronomers make the first record of an eclipse of the Sun.

c 2000 BC
Ancient Britons build Stonehenge, in present-day Wiltshire, as a kind of solar observatory. Stones are aligned to mark points on the horizon where the Sun rises and sets in different seasons, notably at midsummer and midwinter.

585 BC
Thales of Miletus predicts the total eclipse of the Sun on 28 May. The eclipse is so startling that it stops the war being fought between the Medes and the Lydians.

538 BC
First record of a solar eclipse in England, described in the Anglo-Saxon Chronicles.

c 300 BC
Aristarchus suggests that the Earth might circle around the Sun.

c AD 150
Ptolemy writes down all the astronomical knowledge and beliefs of the ancient world, including the idea that the Earth is the centre of the Universe.

600s–1400s
The Mayan, Aztec and Inca civilizations thrive in Central and South America. Sun worship is a major religion.

1600
Giordano Bruno is tortured and burned at the stake for believing in a Solar System, against the teachings of the Church.

1609
Johannes Kepler publishes the first of his three laws of planetary motion. It describes how the planets circle the Sun in elliptical, not circular, orbits.

1610
Galileo first observes sunspots, using the new telescope he has built.

1666
Isaac Newton uses a prism to split white sunlight into a coloured spectrum.

1781
William Herschel discovers a seventh planet, Uranus.

1796
Pierre Laplace puts forward his Nebular Hypothesis, suggesting that the Solar System was born in a cloud of gas in space.

1801
Giovanni Piazzi discovers the first and largest asteroid, Ceries.

1802
William Wollaston first observes the dark lines in the Sun's spectrum.

1814
Josef von Fraunhofer studies the dark lines in the Sun's spectrum, which come to be called Fraunhofer lines.

1836
Francis Baily first observes the 'beads' of light around the Moon, just before total eclipse. They become known as Baily's beads.

1846
Johann Galle discovers the eighth planet, Neptune.

1889
George Hale invents the spectroheliograph, for detailed study of the Sun's spectrum.

1850
Heinrich Schwabe discovers the 11-year sunspot cycle.

1904
Edward Maunder draws the first butterfly diagram, showing how the location of sunspots changes over time.

1905
Albert Einstein introduces his Theory of Relativity, which includes his famous equation $E=mc^2$.

1908
George Hale measures the magnetic field of the Sun.

1919
Studies of the exceptionally long total solar eclipse on 26 May (6 minutes 50 seconds duration) in South America and Africa show that starlight is bent by the Sun's gravity. This effect was predicted by Albert Einstein's General Theory of Relativity (1916).

1930
Clyde Tombaugh discovers the ninth planet, Pluto. Bernard Lyot invents the coronagraph.

1962
The world's largest solar telescope, the McMath, is completed at Kitt Peak National Observatory in Arizona.

1973
Skylab space station launched. Major objective is to study the Sun.

1995
SOHO probe launched to study the Sun. Discovers 'sunquakes' and spots comets diving into the surface.

1999
Total solar eclipse visible across northern Europe and central and southern Asia on 11 August.

2186
On 16 July, a total solar eclipse will take place, of 7 minutes 29 seconds, nearly the longest possible.

NOTHING BUT THE FACTS

Sun data

Diameter at equator	1 392 000 km
Average distance from Earth	149 000 000 km
Volume (Earth's volume = 1)	1 304 000
Mass (Earth's mass = 1)	330 000
Density (water's density = 1)	1.4
Temperature on surface	5500°C
Temperature in centre	15 000 000°C
Spins on axis in	25 days
Star type	yellow dwarf (G2)
Circles round galaxy in	225 000 000 Earth-years
Distance from centre of galaxy	25 000 light-years

Sun and the planets

Planet	Average distance from Sun (million km)	Circles Sun in (d = Earth-days, y = Earth-years)
Mercury	58	88 d
Venus	108.2	224.7 d
Earth	149.6	365.25 d
Mars	227.9	687 d
Jupiter	778.3	11.9 y
Saturn	1427	29.5 y
Uranus	2870	84 y
Neptune	4497	164.8 y
Pluto	5900	247.7 y

Sizes of the planets

Planet	Diameter at equator (km)	Volume (Earth's volume = 1)	Mass (Earth's mass = 1)
Mercury	4878	0.05	0.06
Venus	12 104	0.82	0.88
Earth	12 756	1	1
Mars	6794	0.15	0.11
Jupiter	142 200	1,320	318
Saturn	120 000	744	95
Uranus	51 200	67	15
Neptune	49 500	57	17
Pluto	2284	0.0005	0.002

People file

Name	Nationality	Dates
Aristarchus	Greek	(310-230 BC)
Francis Baily	English	(1774-1844)
Nicolaus Copernicus	Polish	(1473-1543
Albert Einstein	German/US	(1879-1955)
Joseph von Fraunhofer	German	(1787-1826)
Galileo	Italian	(1564-1642)
Johann Galle	German	(1812-1910)
William Herschel	English	(1738-1822)
George Hale	US	(1868-1938)
Johannes Kepler	German	(1571-1630)
Pierre Laplace	French	(1749-1827)
Bernard Lyot	French	(1897-1953)
Edward Maunder	English	(1851-1928)
Isaac Newton	English	(1642-1727)
Giovanni Piazzi	Italian	(1746-1926)
Ptolemy	Greek	(c AD 150)
Heinrich Schwabe	German	(1789-1875)
Thales of Miletus	Greek	(c 640-560 BC)
Clyde Tombaugh	US	(1906-present)

AT THE SPEED OF LIGHT

Light from the Sun takes about 8½ minutes to reach the Earth, but over 4¼ years to reach the nearest star.

ELEMENTARY

The Sun contains more than 70 out of the 90 or so elements found naturally on Earth.

DISCOVERY

The element helium was discovered in the Sun before it was discovered on Earth.

PASSING THROUGH

Every second, more than a million million particles called neutrinos, given off by the Sun, pass through our bodies without doing us any harm.

BLOWING A GALE

The solar wind streams away from the Sun at speeds of up to 3 000 000 km an hour.

MASSIVE

The Sun contains 99.9 per cent of all the mass in the Solar System, totalling about 2000 million million million million tonnes.

SOME SPOT

The biggest sunspot ever was observed in April 1947, measuring about 300 000 km long and 145 000 km wide.

BURNING QUESTION

If the Sun were made up of glowing coal, it would burn itself out in 1500 years.

FAST MOVER

The Sun hurtles through space at a speed of about 250 kilometres a second.

REPEAT PERFORMANCE

The Sun, the Moon and the Earth return to the same relative positions in space after a period of 18 years 11 days. This period, called the saros, has been known since Babylonian times.

FLEETING SHADOW

During a solar eclipse, the Moon's shadow races across the Earth's surface at a speed of more than 3000 km an hour.

THE END

In 5-6 billion years, the Sun will stop shining. By then it will have shrunk into a black dwarf star about the size of the Earth.

GLOSSARY

asteroids
Lumps of rock that orbit the Sun in a band between the orbits of Mars and Jupiter.

astrology
A belief that people's lives are affected by the planets and the stars.

astronomy
The scientific study of the stars.

atmosphere
A layer of gases around a planet or a star.

aurora
A display of coloured lights in far northern and far southern skies.

axis
An imaginary line around which a body spins.

calendar
A means of dividing up the year into months, weeks and days.

chemical elements
The basic chemicals found in all kinds of substances; the building blocks of matter.

chromosphere
The Sun's coloured inner atmosphere.

climate
The typical weather of a place during the year.

comet
An icy ball of matter that starts to glow when it nears the Sun.

constellation
A group of bright stars that appear in the same part of the sky.

corona
The white outer atmosphere of the Sun.

coronagraph
An instrument that shows up the Sun's corona.

cosmic year
The time the Sun takes to travel once around the centre of our galaxy.

day
The time the Earth takes to spin round once in space.

eclipse
When one heavenly body passes in front of another and blocks its light.

ecliptic
The path the Sun seems to follow among the stars, as viewed from the Earth.

elements
see chemical elements

Equator
An imaginary line around the Earth, midway between the North and South Poles.

equinox
A time of the year when the hours of daylight and night-time are the same.

flare
A sudden outburst of energy on the Sun.

fusion
A process in which atoms join together.

galaxy
A great star 'island' in space, containing many billions of stars.

gravity
The force that attracts one lump of matter to another.

leap year
A year 366 days long, one day more than the ordinary calendar year.

light-year
A unit astronomers use to measure distances in space. It equals the distance light travels in a year – about 10 million million km.

moon
A natural satellite of a planet.

nuclear reaction
A process that involves the nuclei (centres) of atoms. Nuclear fusion is a reaction in which the nuclei of atoms join together.

orbit
The path in space a body follows when it circles around another.

ozone layer
A layer of a gas called ozone, found high in the Earth's atmosphere.

photosphere
The bright outer surface of the Sun.

photosynthesis
The process green plants use to make their food in daylight.

planet
A large body that circles in space around the Sun.

prominence
A fountain of flaming gas that rises through the Sun's atmosphere.

satellite
A body or an object that circles around another body in space. The Moon is a natural satellite of the Earth. The Earth also has many artificial satellites.

season
A period of the year when temperatures and the weather are much the same as in previous years.

solar
To do with the Sun.

solar cell
An electronic device that changes sunlight directly into electricity.

solar eclipse
An eclipse of the Sun.

Solar System
The Sun's family, which includes the planets and their moons, asteroids and comets.

solar wind
A stream of particles given out by the Sun.

spectrum
A spread of colours created when sunlight passes through a prism, or wedge of glass.

star
A huge ball of hot gases, which gives off energy as light, heat and other radiation.

sundial
A device that measures the time when the Sun is out by the position of the shadow of a pointer on a dial.

sunspot
A dark patch on the Sun's surface.

total eclipse
The moment during an eclipse of the Sun when the Moon totally covers the Sun and makes the sky dark.

Universe
Everything that exists – the Earth, space, stars and planets.

year
The time the Earth takes to circle once in space around the Sun.

zodiac
An imaginary band in the heavens in which the Sun and the planets are found.

INDEX